I0797705

Amazing Young People

WOLFGANG AMADEUS MOZART

Martha London

DiscoverRoo
An Imprint of Pop!
popbooksonline.com

abdobooks.com

Published by Pop!, a division of ABDO, PO Box 398166, Minneapolis, Minnesota 55439.

Printed in the United States of America, North Mankato, Minnesota

052019
092019

THIS BOOK CONTAINS RECYCLED MATERIALS

Cover Photo: iStockphoto

Interior Photos: iStockphoto, 1, 12, 13 (top), 13 (bottom), 19, 23 (bottom), 30, 31; North Wind Picture Archives, 5, 14–15, 17; akg-images/Newscom, 6; Shutterstock Images, 7, 18, 20–21, 22 (left), 29; Music-Images/Lebrecht Music & Arts/Alamy, 8, 25; FineArt/Alamy, 9; World History Archive/Newscom, 11; Album/Fine Art Images/Newscom, 22 (right); Kerstin Joensson/AP Images, 23 (top); Album/Scottish National Portrait Gallery/Newscom, 26; Album/Alamy, 27; Ivy Close Images/Alamy, 28

Editor: Brienna Rossiter

Series Designer: Sarah Taplin

Library of Congress Control Number: 2018964790

Publisher's Cataloging-in-Publication Data

Names: London, Martha, author.

Title: Wolfgang Amadeus Mozart / by Martha London.

Description: Minneapolis, Minnesota : Pop!, 2020 | Series: Amazing young people | Includes online resources and index.

Identifiers: ISBN 9781532163715 (lib. bdg.) | ISBN 9781644940440 (pbk.) | ISBN 9781532165153 (ebook)

Subjects: LCSH: Mozart, Wolfgang Amadeus, 1756-1791--Juvenile literature. | Composers--Austria--Biography--Juvenile literature. | Composers--Biography--Juvenile literature. | Musicians--Biography--Juvenile literature.

Classification: DDC 780.92 [B]--dc23

WELCOME TO DiscoverRoo!

Pop open this book and you'll find QR codes loaded with information, so you can learn even more!

Scan this code* and others like it while you read, or visit the website below to make this book pop!

popbooksonline.com/wolfgang-amadeus-mozart

*Scanning QR codes requires a web-enabled smart device with a QR code reader app and a camera.

TABLE OF CONTENTS

CHAPTER 1
A MUSICAL GENIUS

Wolfgang Amadeus Mozart was a famous **composer**. He was born in Austria in 1756. Mozart was a **prodigy**. He began playing and writing music when he was very young.

WATCH A VIDEO HERE!

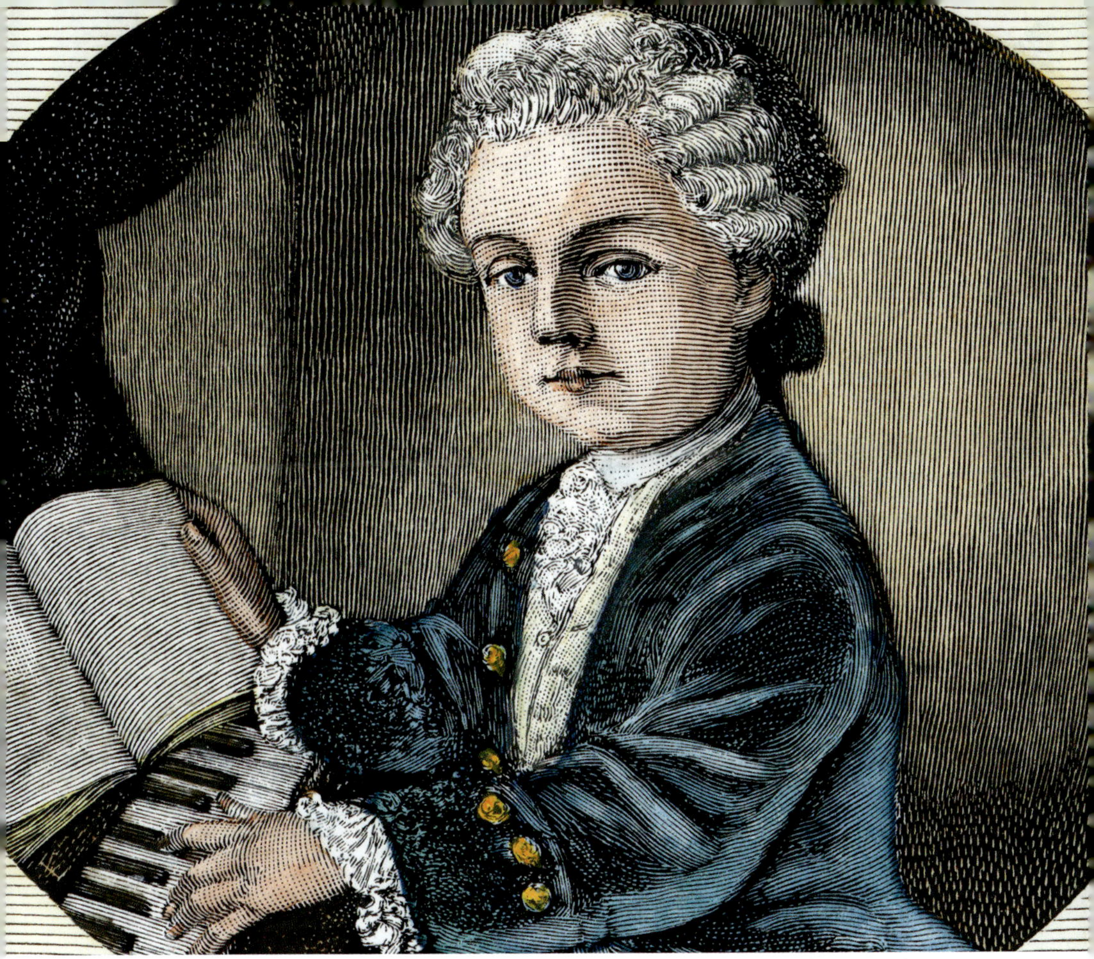

From an early age, Wolfgang Amadeus Mozart showed great musical talent.

Mozart wrote his first piece of music when he was only five years old.

Courts often had their own stages where singers and musicians performed.

In the 1700s, most composers worked for a **court** or a church. Mozart was different. He made money by

Mozart was born in this house in Salzburg, Austria.

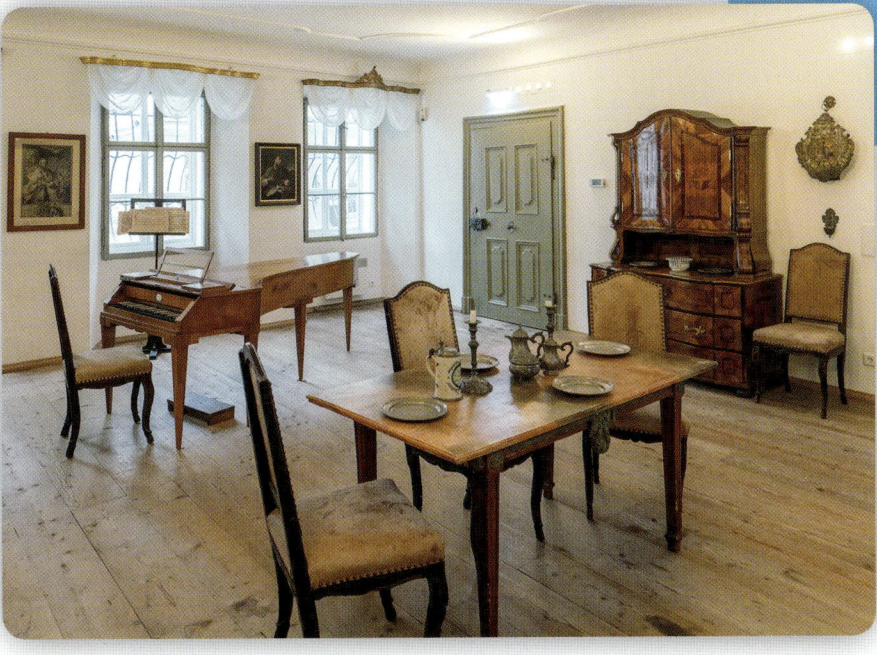

teaching lessons, playing concerts, and writing lots and lots of music.

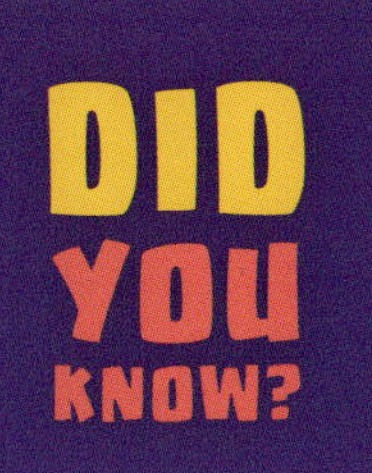

Mozart wrote more than 600 pieces of music during his life. By age 15, he had written more than 100 pieces.

Most composers focused on just one kind of music. Some wrote **sonatas** or **symphonies**. Others wrote **operas**. Mozart wrote many different kinds of music. And he had success in all of them. Many people think he was one of the greatest composers ever.

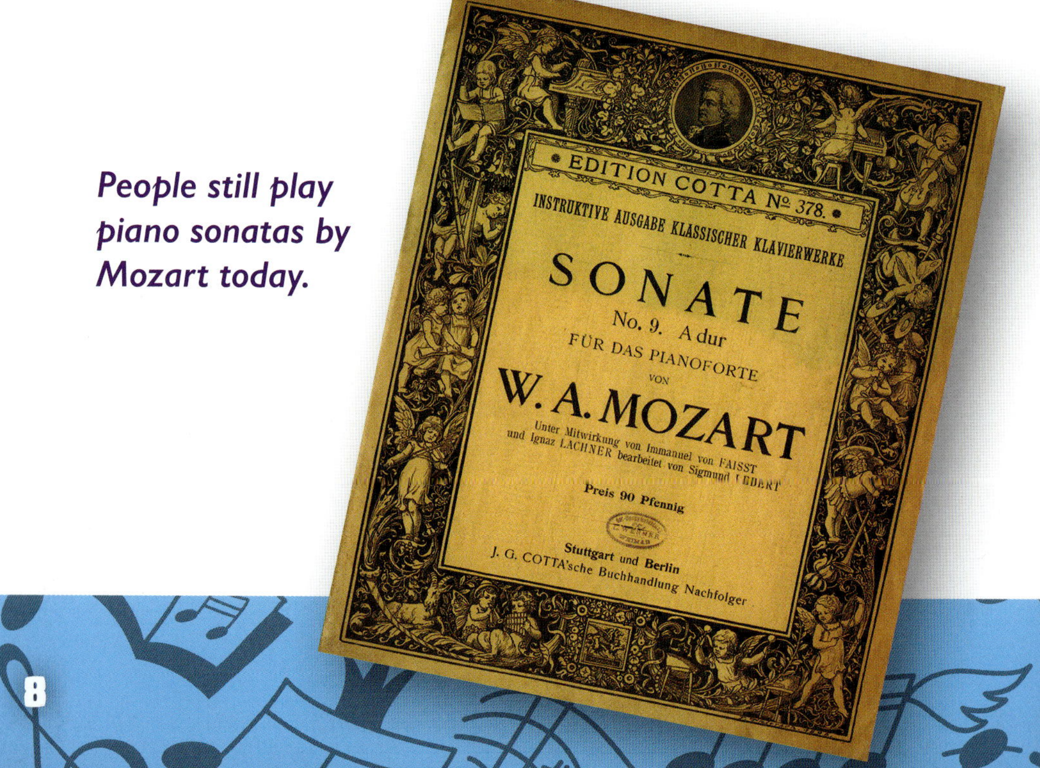

People still play piano sonatas by Mozart today.

Mozart wrote many famous operas, sonatas, and symphonies.

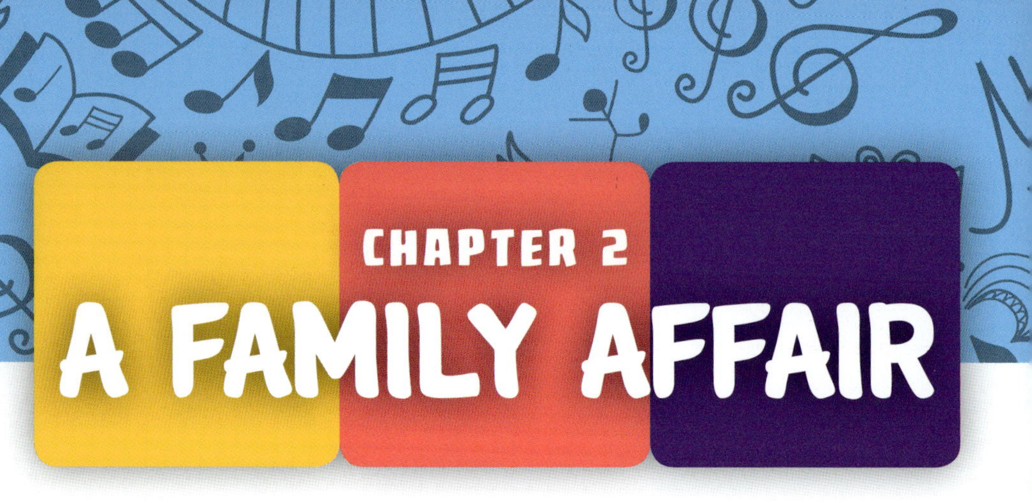

CHAPTER 2
A FAMILY AFFAIR

Wolfgang Amadeus Mozart was born on January 27, 1756. He lived in Salzburg, Austria. Wolfgang came from a musical family. His father, Leopold, was a **composer**. He taught music lessons to

A young Wolfgang plays music with his father and sister.

Wolfgang's older sister. Her name was Maria Anna, or "Nannerl" for short.

One day when Wolfgang was three years old, he began playing along. After that, Leopold gave music lessons to both his children. Wolfgang learned to play violin and organ. He also played harpsichord. This keyboard instrument was similar to a piano.

KEYBOARD INSTRUMENTS

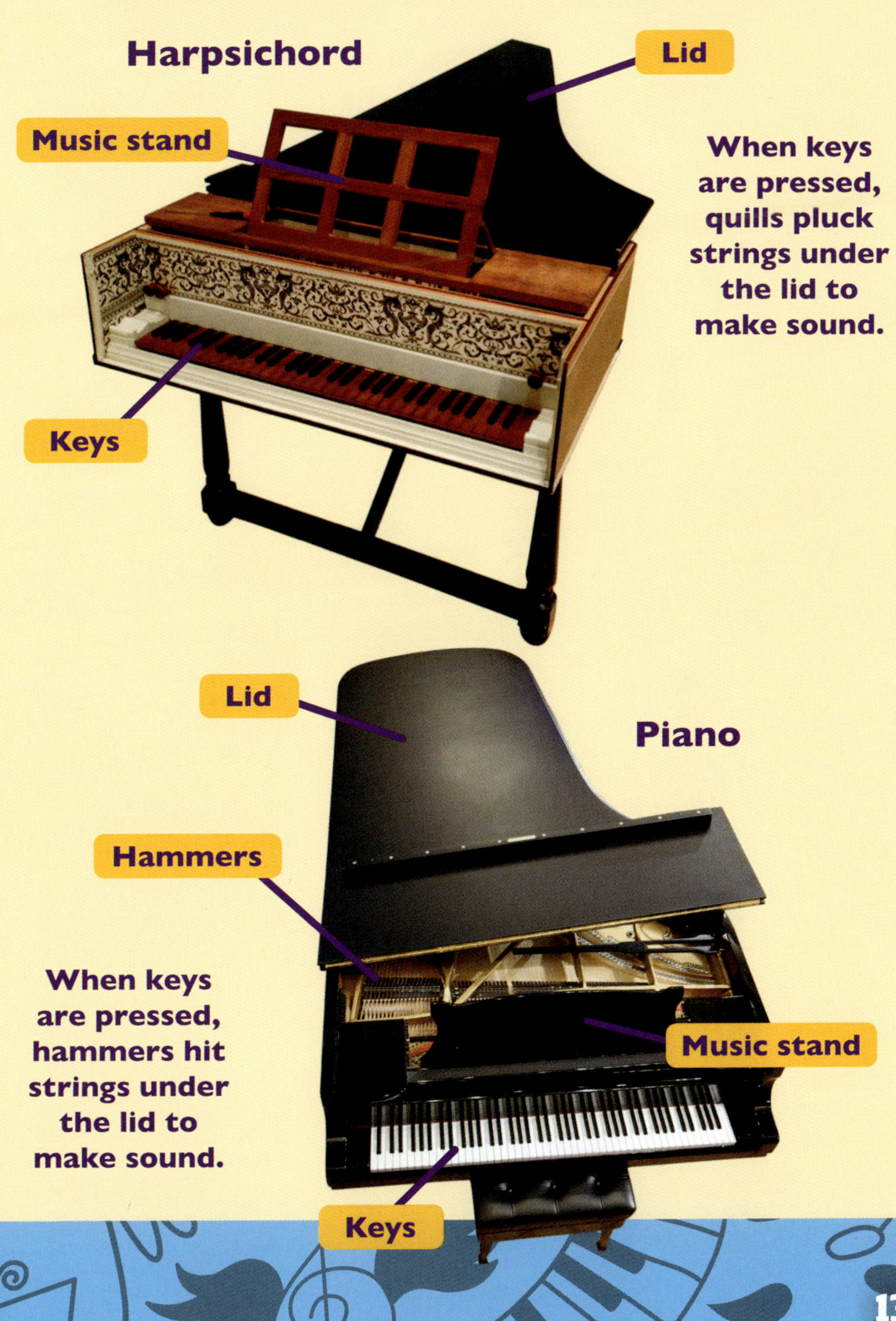

When keys are pressed, quills pluck strings under the lid to make sound.

When keys are pressed, hammers hit strings under the lid to make sound.

Wolfgang and Nannerl played for Empress Maria Theresa of Austria in 1762.

In 1763, the Mozart family began traveling all over Europe. Wolfgang and Nannerl played concerts at parties, palaces, and churches. Wolfgang began

writing music too. He learned new ideas and styles in each city he visited.

MANY MUSICAL SKILLS

From a young age, Wolfgang was a talented musician. He could play whole pieces after hearing them a single time. Once, he even wrote out all the different parts sung by a choir. Wolfgang was also famous for his ability to improvise. That means making up music on the spot.

CHAPTER 3
MANY KINDS OF MUSIC

Mozart moved to Vienna, Austria, in 1781. He continued giving many concerts. He also wrote lots of new music. Mozart often played the piano. So, he wrote **sonatas** and other piano pieces.

COMPLETE AN ACTIVITY HERE!

Mozart often wrote new music to perform on the piano at concerts.

A conductor leads musicians as they play.

Mozart also wrote music for orchestras. He often **conducted** the performances. Some pieces were **symphonies**. Others were concertos.

In a concerto, a solo instrument plays along with an orchestra. Mozart wrote music for small groups of musicians too.

DID YOU KNOW?

Mozart wrote 27 piano concertos. He also wrote concertos for other instruments, including violin.

In the 1780s, Mozart began focusing more on **opera**. He wrote a total of 22 operas during his life. The last four

Singers perform The Marriage of Figaro*, an opera Mozart wrote in 1786.*

operas are the most famous, especially *The Magic Flute*. Mozart finished this opera in September 1791.

TIMELINE

1756

Wolfgang Amadeus Mozart is born in Salzburg, Austria, on January 27.

1759

Leopold begins giving Wolfgang music lessons.

1763

Wolfgang leaves Salzburg to travel around Europe for his first concert tour.

1767

Wolfgang completes his first opera.

1788

Mozart writes three symphonies in one year. They are some of his best works.

1791

Mozart dies on December 5.

CHAPTER 4
ALL AROUND THE WORLD

In the fall of 1791, Mozart was working on a piece of music called the *Requiem*. But he became very sick. He died before finishing it. Mozart was only 35. Yet he was already famous all over Europe.

Mozart worked on composing right up until his death.

Music for small groups of performers is called chamber music. Musicians often played it in rooms of palaces or homes.

Mozart wrote almost every kind of music that existed. He helped improve several forms, such as the **sonata**. And he explored new things music could do. His music shows a wide range of feelings.

Mozart wrote his music, such as this string quartet, by hand.

Young composer Ludwig van Beethoven performs for Mozart.

Many later **composers** studied his work. They wrote music that expressed even more emotion. Mozart's music

People attend concerts to hear Mozart's music performed.

continues to be popular today. People all over the world play and listen to it.

Mozart wrote *Eine Kleine Nachtmusik* in 1787. It's still one of the most popular pieces of classical music.

MAKING CONNECTIONS

TEXT-TO-SELF

Mozart loved music from a young age. What is something you enjoyed when you were little?

TEXT-TO-TEXT

Have you read other books about musicians or composers? What kind of music did they play or write?

TEXT-TO-WORLD

Mozart composed music long ago. Why do you think people still play and listen to it today?

GLOSSARY

composer – a person who writes music.

conduct – to lead a group of musicians as they sing or play.

court – the home of a ruler (such as a king) and the people who live and work there.

opera – a play where most words are sung.

prodigy – someone who develops a skill at a very young age.

sonata – a form of classical music made up of several sections played by one instrument.

symphony – a form of classical music made up of several sections played by an orchestra.

INDEX

Scan this code* and others like it while you read, or visit the website below to make this book pop!

popbooksonline.com/wolfgang-amadeus-mozart

*Scanning QR codes requires a web-enabled smart device with a QR code reader app and a camera.